# Success with
# Your
# Herb Garden

## HEIDE RAU

Series Editor
### LESLEY YOUNG

MEREHURST

# Contents

**Foreword**

A small bunch of parsley here, a few chives there – your garden need not look as dull as that. Herbs can be combined in many delightful ways – with each other but also with vegetables, flowers and fruit. In addition, they bring colour and scent to the garden, a delicious flavour to your cooking and they also contain many health-promoting substances. In this colourful guide, author Heide Rau will introduce you to the world of herbs and show you just how useful they can be.

There is a section on designing with herbs, which includes a host of ideas on how to transform your garden. For example, how about a scented path, a herb staircase or herbs as a centrepiece to a flowerbed?

The practical sections contain easy-to-follow instructions, even for beginners, and information and advice on all the important aspects of herbs and their care. This includes tips and suggestions on harvesting, preserving and use. Lovely colour photographs by well-known plant photographer Marion Nickig will tempt you to have a go at creating a herb garden of your own which will become a veritable feast for the senses.

*A charming arrangement of herbs in the front garden.*

*Comfrey flower.*

*Butterflies love herbs.*

**The author**
Heide Rau is a teacher of biology and history. As a dedicated herb gardener, she also lectures on the growing and use of herbs and grows a very wide range of different herb species and varieties in her own garden.

**Acknowledgements**
The author wishes to thank Heike Kleineweischede for her ideas and for reading the manuscript; also Daniel Rühlemann and Burghart Koch for invaluable suggestions.

**The photographer**
Marion Nickig has become well known for her unusual garden and flower photographs. She has worked for many well-known garden and interior decorating magazines over the last ten years.

NB: Please read the Author's Note on page 63.

# The wide range of herbs

Nowadays, herbs from all over the world can be found in many European gardens, while old-fashioned plants that our grandmothers knew well are being cultivated again, side by side with exotic and rare plants that they never dreamed of. From the oyster plant to lemon balm, you will be amazed at the sheer variety of the world of herbs!

*Photo above: Sage flowers hold precious nectar for visiting honeybees and bumble bees.*
*Photo left: Herbs with many different colours of leaves and shapes of growth can look most effective. A gooseberry standard and spherical, clipped box trees are the elements which provide order in this lively arrangement.*

# The wide range of herbs

## All about herbs

Herbs are fascinating, attractive plants. Fortunately, you do not have to have the proverbial "green fingers" to cultivate them as they are very easy to grow. They grow fast, are usually resistant to most diseases and are beneficial for humans, animals and other plants. Everyone ought to have at least a few herbs in the garden to enjoy their flavour, scent and beauty.

Knowledge of the many useful properties of herbs has been accumulated over thousands of years and much of this lore has been confirmed by modern scientific investigation. Folk legends of wise women and hermits skilled in the knowledge of the healing properties of herbs permeate the history of many cultures. These historical echoes make herbs even more fascinating and are part of the attraction that induces people to grow these pleasant-smelling, tasty, healing herbs, whether they are used as medicinal plants for teas and tisanes, for infusions or inhaling, in cooking for seasoning countless dishes or as ornamental plants that fill the garden with a wonderful scent.

## What are herbs?

The plants that we normally refer to as herbs are characterized by their content of substances with certain properties. Botanically, they are quite a mixed bunch.

**Annuals** are sown in the spring, produce seeds in the same year and die back in the autumn. Among these herbs are dill (*Anethum graveolens*) and borage (*Borago officinalis*).

**Biennials** flower and produce fruit in the second year after sowing. If only the leaves are wanted, as with parsley (*Petroselinum crispum*), you can harvest in the same year as sowing. If you want to use the seeds, as with caraway (*Carum carvi*), you can leave the plant to overwinter and then produce flowers.

**Perennials** are plants whose parts above ground die off in the winter while the root overwinters in the soil. Among these are chives (*Allium schoenoprasum*), lovage (*Levisticum officinale*) and peppermint (*Mentha piperita*).

**Semi-shrubs** are perennial plants whose lower parts become woody, for example, lavender (*Lavandula angustifolia*).

**Shrubs** are perennial woody plants. In this group there are several species containing effective substances. Rosemary (*Rosmarinus officinalis*) and elder (*Sambucus nigra*) are well-known examples.

***The consituents of herbs:*** The following effective substances can be found in varying proportions in all herbs:
- bitter substances and tannins
- colourings
- mucilage
- etheric oils
- saponins
- glycosides
- alkaloids
- vitamins
- minerals
- trace elements

## Too much of anything is not good for your health:

Many substances which can have a beneficial effect on health if taken in very small doses, may actually be harmful or even toxic if taken in high doses. It is therefore vital to stay away from well-known toxic plants like foxglove (*Digitalis* species) or deadly nightshade (*Atropa belladonna*), whose toxicity is great enough to cause death if consumed. This volume is limited to herbs that are not harmful if consumed in sensible quantities and are actually beneficial to health (see Author's Note, p. 63).

*Herbs will bring scent and colour to your garden, for example brilliantly coloured marigolds and scented lavender.*

## Why are herbs scented?

The typical scent of herbs relates to their content of etheric oils. These are found in the flowers as well as in the leaves. Very often, it is the scent of the leaves that is stronger. In the case of some plants, however, it is specifically the flowers that we gather, for example lavender, chamomile and St. John's wort. On warm, sunny days during the summer, the volatile etheric oils of herbs become particularly obvious through their strong, pleasant odour and after a warm summer shower the air in the garden is filled with their scent. The scent molecules are released through the action of wind or touch and combine with oxygen to produce the perfumes we recognize. With some herbs, on the other hand, the leaves or flowers have to be rubbed between one's fingers to release the scent.

**My tip:** If you are a newcomer to herb gardening, you should make a point of frequently rubbing, smelling and tasting your herbs in order to get to know them.

# The wide range of herbs

Herb flowers are delicate works of art created by nature. Some of these beauties are best appreciated close up, like this pink and white flower of Leonurus cardiaca.

## The beauty of flowering herbs

The flowers of herbs are not as spectacular as those of highly cultivated flower hybrids that are raised to be ever larger, more beautiful and more colourful. The delicate herb flowers in their pastel shades are much shyer beauties whose natural charm is realized in combination with other flowers. Lavender (*Lavandula angustifolia*), sage (*Salvia officinalis*) and thyme (*Thymus vulgaris*) greatly enhance the romantic character of roses and other shrubs without being conspicuous themselves.

Of course, there are some herbs with very colourful flowers, such as bergamot (*Monarda didyma*) in brilliant shades of red, or the golden orange marigold (*Calendula officinalis*). They look good in beds with other colourful summer flowers but will also provide a cheerful accent in a herb garden.

### Shapes and colours

The flowers of herbs are extremely varied. There are:
● single flowers coloured yellow, red or orange, such as nasturtium (*Tropaeolum majus*)
● daisy-like flowers coloured orange and yellow, like marigold (*Calendula officinalis*)
● the blue spikes of lavender (*Lavandula angustifolia*)
● the blue flowery racemes of sage (*Salvia officinalis*) or those in white, such as lemon balm (*Melissa officinalis*)
● the yellow umbels of fennel (*Foeniculum vulgare*) or the white ones of caraway (*Carum carvi*).

### An invitation to insects

Of course, neither the colour of the flowers nor the scent is meant for humans. They have evolved to send out signals to insects that here will be found a store laden with pollen and nectar. Honeybees, bumble bees and butterflies fly busily from one flower to another, collecting tiny drops of nectar. At the same time, they are making possible the pollination of the flowers by transporting pollen from one plant to another. Butterflies like lavender, thyme and sage. Their favourite plant, however, is oregano (*Origanum vulgare*) (see p. 45) where honeybees and bumble bees are also frequent visitors. In a herb garden the warm hours around midday are a favourite time for many insects.

**My tip:** Oregano, which flowers in high summer and scatters seed plentifully, can be planted all over the garden. In this way you will be able to enjoy the sight of butterflies fluttering around the whole garden, filling it with life.

## Herb flowers in cooking

A new trend in the "green" kitchen is a great variety of salads, desserts and soups decorated with edible flowers. Favourites for salads are the flowers of chives, fennel, marigold and nasturtium. Sage, lavender and the glowing red flowers of bergamot (*Monarda*) are used for desserts. As a rule, the flowers do not have such a strong taste as the leaves and are thus more subtle for seasoning. If you think eating flowers is rather an unusual idea, think of the flowers in chamomile tea and the large "flowers" of such vegetables as cauliflower, broccoli and artichokes, all of which are eaten without qualms. Our grandmothers often used flowers in cooking, for example candied violets, marzipan made with rosewater and nasturtium flowers in salads.

Nowadays, many of these customs have been forgotten and people must learn again to use the great variety of nature's treasures. You do not need to buy exotic fruits to turn fruit salad and desserts into works of art – just use a few herb flowers!

*A traditional herb garden with a classical path layout, box edging and central roundel.*

## Historical herb gardens

The first recorded mention of herb gardens is derived from the reign of Charlemagne (AD 742-814) in whose famous estate roll, the "Capitulare de Villis", one can read lists of many herbs, used for healing and culinary purposes, that are still in use today.

Charlemagne's tenants were encouraged to plant herbs like chervil, dill, savory, fennel, tarragon, mint, lovage, rosemary and many more on his country estates. Lilies, iris, mallow and roses are also recorded in the lists. They were not planted and grown merely for their beauty, however, but also for use in medicinal preparations.

Herb gardens were expected to look attractive as aesthetic considerations were important in the old monastery gardens and country estates. Only a few of the ancient herb gardens have survived but many of the basic ideas on which they were formulated have been passed on through the generations to be resurrected in modern herb gardens. If you have sufficient room in your garden, you cannot go wrong with the creation of a traditional herb garden.

## A traditional herb garden

● Walls or hedges grown from yew (very toxic!) or privet will provide a visual screen and a windbreak. They also create boundaries and separate different parts of the garden from each other. Hedges give structure to a garden, even in winter when the herbs are in their dormant phase.

● The centre of the herb garden may feature a sundial, the calming sound of a trickling fountain, a bird bath, a spherically cut box tree or a standard gooseberry or rose bush. This will continue to provide interest for the onlooker, even in winter.

● From the centre, paths lead into the herb garden proper, demarcating the various sections. The classical division is a crosspath (see p. 12) creating four beds that surround a circular flowerbed or roundel in the centre.

● Dividing each bed up into several more is a very practical way to design individual sections. Triangular beds are easy to get at and see into.

● The beds themselves are often edged with low box tree borders which provide a sheltered mini-climate for the herbs and also show the flowering plants off to good advantage.

● A seat placed in a herb garden is a constant invitation to take time off.

## The herb "renaissance"

Medieval traditions of herb growing and classical herb gardens have become fashionable again in the twentieth century. A reconsideration of old healing traditions and a growing scepticism about synthetically produced pharmaceuticals have created a renewed interest in herbs. Not only as healing plants but also as flavourings in cooking, these plants are enjoying a veritable renaissance. Gourmet chefs now season their five-star creations with herbs and dedicated amateurs follow suit. In order to do likewise, you will need either a very well-stocked local market or, better still, you can grow your own herbs in your garden. You do not have to install a complete medieval herb garden, of course, as even a single bed will enrich both your garden and your menu.

# Classical shapes of beds

### A simple cross

A central crosspath is the basis for the simplest form of herb garden. A potentially fairly severe-looking plan is enclosed by low walls or hedges, all with straight lines and evergreen box borders that give a sense of peace and order.

### Rhomboid

Symmetrically designed triangular beds are integrated into an attractive diamond shape. The beds should not be wider than 1 m (40 in) so that the herbs are easily accessible from all sides. Fine pea gravel is attractive for the paths; natural stone paving slabs or bricks also look good.

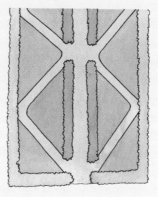

### Cruciform with roundel

The roundel at the crossing point of the two paths gives this ancient monastic design its appeal. The visual point at the centre can be a fountain, a sundial or a round bed planted with herbs and roses.

### A fruit garden with herbs

Fruit trees trained as espaliers can easily be combined with herbs. Both fruit and herbs will develop their scent and flavour during warm summer days. Sun-warmed pears served with fresh soft cheese and herbs make an appetizing combination for lunch! This type of garden should be well protected behind stone walls covered with climbing plants and creepers.

### A rustic garden

A rustic garden aims to look much less formal than a classical one. Here, flowering plants can spill out of the beds during the summer, allowing plants such as marigolds, borage and mullein to glow in colourful competition with each other. Such a mixture will look both luxuriant and cheerful at the same time.

### Individual herb beds

For people with a busy lifestyle, a herb bed on or near a patio will be ideal. This will save long trips across the garden and you will end up using your herbs more often because they are easy to get at. Further advantages include:
● The stone-flagged patio will radiate warmth to the herbs. This is particularly appreciated by Mediterranean herbs whose flavour will be more intense if they grow in a sunny and very dry place.

*A modern herb garden with a colourful, mixed planting. Structure is provided by the rather severe spherical box trees.*

● If the patio is surrounded by walls, you have the same situation as in a monastery garden: a place of peace and relaxation and the scent of the herbs will be retained within the four walls.

● Herb beds need not be square. Dividing them up into segments (like slices of a cake, for example) is both attractive and practical.

**My tip:** Plant strongly scented herbs as close as possible to paths that are often used. Every time you brush past them, and with every gust of wind, you can enjoy their lovely scent, like a form of wind-borne aromatherapy!

***Further examples*** of designing with herbs, roses, flowers and even with vegetables can be found in the section on designing with herbs (see p. 27). There can hardly be any garden where herbs are unable to play an enhancing role.

All you have to do is to allow yourself to be enchanted by the ambience created by them.

**My tip:** There are a number of private gardens in Britain, the Netherlands and Belgium which are well worth visiting and where you will be able to admire many different designs of herb garden.

*1 Lovage.*

# Popular herbs for the kitchen

The variety of well-known and well-loved herbs for cooking that is indispensable in any garden ranges from parsley and chives, which most people have, to old favourites that have recently been rediscovered, like stonecrop (*Sedum reflexum*) and salad burnet.

*2 Chives form attractive, pinkish-violet, almost spherical flowerheads.*

3 Salad burnet is a graceful perennial that will remain green throughout the winter.

5 Tarragon can grow 1.5 m (60 in) tall.

4 White-flowering chervil.

6 Borage has blue star-shaped flowers.

## 1 Lovage
*Levisticum officinale*
(photograph, p. 14)

A hardy, undemanding seasoning herb.
**Origin:** Southern Europe.
**Appearance:** 180-200 cm (72-80 in) tall. Shiny, green, coarsely feathery leaves, aromatic smell. Yellowish-green flowers in the first to second months of summer. **Position:** Semi-shady. Nutrient-rich, moist soil. **Care:** Fertilize with ripe compost. Undemanding. **Use:** Fresh or dried leaves in soups, stews. Young leaves in salad dressings and with potatoes. The seeds can be used in breadmaking and in pies. **Design:** Lovage looks good around the edge of a vegetable garden or herb bed. It will also fit into semi-shady borders with bushes and shrubs.

## 2 Chives
*Allium schoenoprasum*
(photograph, p. 14)

Hardy perennial with decorative, spherical flowers.
**Varieties:** Chives with thick stems
(*A. schoenoprasum* "Grolau").
**Origin:** Europe, Asia.
**Appearance:** 15-30 cm (6-12 in) tall. Grass-like leaves. Pinkish-violet flowers during the first and second months of summer. **Position:** Sunny

# The wide range of herbs

to semi-shady. Nutrient-rich,
slightly moist soil.
**Care:** Sow seed or divide clump.
**Use:** Popular herb in soups,
sauces, with vegetables. The
flowers have a milder flavour than
the leaves, pretty when pulled
apart and sprinkled on salads
and herb butter. Only use fresh.
Suitable for freezing. **Design:** As
an edging plant along borders
and with roses.
**My tip:** Many other *Allium*
species have similar requirements
and use, for example
*A. tuberosum* "Knolau" or
*A. fistulosum*, a winter hedge
plant.

### 3 Salad burnet
*Sanguisorba minor*
(photograph, p. 15)

Delicate perennial.
**Origin:** Central and southern
Europe.
**Appearance:** 30-40 cm (12-16
in) tall. Oval, single, feathery
leaves with dentate edges,
spherical red flowers on long
stems.
**Position:** Sunny to semi-shady.
Dry, lime-rich soil. **Care:** Remove
inflorescences before the flowers
open. Cut back frequently so
young leaves can continue
growing. **Use:** A fresh taste of
cucumber and nuts. With salads,
salmon, eggs, soups, sauces and
in cold drinks. Freezing possible.
**Design:** Salad burnet remains
green during the winter. Plant in a
herb garden or vegetable bed.
Good at the front of a flowerbed
because of its attractive leaves.

*7 Sedum reflexum.*

*8 Yellow green ginger mint.*

*9 Lemon balm.*

### 4 Chervil
*Anthriscus cerefolium*
(photograph, p. 15)

Dainty, annual seasoning herb.
**Origin:** South-eastern Europe.
**Appearance:** 30-50 cm (12-20
in) tall. Soft, feathery, small
leaves. White flowers in first
month of summer. **Position:**
Semi-shady. Moist soil. **Care:** Will
only germinate in temperatures
below 15°C (59°F). Light-
germinating species. If grown in a
favourable position, it will seed
itself. **Use:** The small leaves have
a faint taste of aniseed and are
good with salads, eggs, cheese,
salmon. Popular as chervil soup
and will add a special flavour to
potato soup. Delicate, young
leaves should be used before the
plant flowers. Freezing possible.
**Design:** Chervil grown among
other plants will keep slugs
and snails away. Will grow well
in a pot.

### 5 Tarragon
*Artemisia dracunculus*
(photograph, p. 15)

Hardy perennial with strong
flavour.
**Origin:** South and central Asia.
**Appearance:** 60-150 cm (24-60
in) tall. Bushy, branching stems
with small, narrow leaves. Myrtle-
like, light green flowers from late
summer to mid-autumn.
**Position:** Sunny to semi-shady.
Humus-rich, fresh soil. **Use:** A
fine seasoning for tomatoes,
salads, sauces and herb butter.
Excellent for flavouring vinegar.
Only use fresh; drying is not
recommended. Freezing is
possible. **Design:** Goes well with
compact plants, for example sage.

Will also look good in front of a climbing rose.
**My tip:** *A. dracunculus* var. *sativa*, or French tarragon, is particularly flavourful.

## 6 Borage
*Borago officinalis*
(photograph, p. 15)

Decorative, annual herb with sky blue, star-shaped flowers. *Origin:* Southern Europe. *Appearance:* 50-80 cm (20-32 in) tall. Usually blue, sometimes pink, flowers from early summer to autumn. Oval, rough, hairy leaves. *Position:* Sunny, will cope with a little shade. All types of soil. *Care:* Self-sowing. *Use:* Tastes a little like cucumber when fresh. Chopped leaves with salads, with cheese and in sandwiches. Flowers can be used as a decoration on salads and in drinks. Use fresh only. *Design:* Goes well with red or white roses.

## 7 Stonecrop, stone orpine
*Sedum reflexum*
(photograph, p. 16)

Hardy perennial, often used as an ornamental plant in gardens. *Origin:* Central Europe. *Appearance:* 30 cm (12 in) tall. Shoots prostrate with needle-like, bluish-green leaves. Yellow flowers from mid-summer to late summer. *Position:* Sunny. Dry, poor soil. *Care:* Undemanding plant. Propagates from shoots. *Use:* Mild, sour taste. With salads, with butter on new potatoes. *Design:* Ideal for walls and edges of beds. Also attractive in pots.

## 8 Mint
*Mentha* spp
(photograph, p. 16)

Perennial, scented herb.
*Species/varieties:*
● orange mint
(*Mentha piperita* "Citrata")
● peppermint
(*Mentha piperita officinalis*)
● ginger mint
*(Mentha gentilis)*
● (*Mentha gentilis* "Variegata")
● applemint
(*Mentha suaveolens* "Bowles")
*Appearance:* 30-80 cm (12-32 in) tall. The leaves vary, according to the species and variety, from light green to reddish-veined, from white to yellow striped. Attractive, lavender-coloured spikes on "Bowles" applemint. *Origin:* Europe. *Position:* Semi-shady. Slightly moist soil. *Care:* Propagate by dividing. Underground rhizomes can be a nuisance. *Use:* The mints with a strong flavour, *M. piperita* and *citrata,* for tea, the milder ones, *M. gentilis* and *M. suaveolens,* in the kitchen for sauces, vegetables dishes, salads and desserts. *Design:* A scented path with different mint varieties. The striped-leaf varieties look good in a flowerbed. **Warning:** Do not use mint too regularly or in very large quantities. Not for small children!

## 9 Lemon balm
*Melissa officinalis*
(photograph, p. 16)

Hardy perennial smelling of lemon.
*Varieties:* Yellow balm ("Aurea"). *Origin:* Mediterranean countries, Asia Minor. *Appearance:* 50-100 cm (20-40 in) tall. Light green, small leaves, also yellow striped. Flower white, inconspicuous, from early to late summer. *Position:* Full sunlight to slightly shady. Dry as well as moist soil. *Care:* Propagation by division. Self-sowing. *Use:* With vegetables, poultry, fish, salads, in fruit salad and jam. Fresh, delicate leaves can be used any time. Harvest shortly before flowering for dried tea. Freezing possible. *Design:* The delicate lemon balm leaves are very decorative grown beside tough horse radish leaves.

## 10 Savory
*Satureja* spp

A flavourful seasoning herb. *Species:* S. montana, winter savory; *S. hortensis,* summer savory. Origin: Mediterranean countries. *Appearance:* 10-50 cm (4-20 in) tall. Flavoured, narrow, small leaves, slightly rounded in *S. hortensis.* Flower pink to pinkish-violet during early to mid-summer. *Position:* Sunny. Well-drained soil. *Care:* Sow seed of *S. hortensis* in last month of spring. Cut *S. montana* in late spring. Propagation by layering hanging shoots and by cuttings from shoots. Will require some form of winter protection. *Use:* Savory can be used with legumes instead of salt, particularly with beans, also in soups. It is cooked with the dish and makes food easier to digest. Harvest during flowering. Will retain its strong taste when dried. *Design:* S. montana goes well with varieties of thyme and lavender; *S. hortensis* with beans and in the vegetable garden.

*1 Nasturtium.*

# Mediterranean and exotic herbs

Just as the Mediterranean herbs, like sage, rosemary and thyme, were once brought to monastery gardens, so, too, exotic foreign herbs from many different countries of the world are now finding a home in our gardens. Basil and oyster plant, for example, are firm favourites which have added their flavour to our range of herbs in more recent times.

*2 Almost a shrub, bronze fennel grows up to 2 m (80 in) tall.*

3 Rosemary has delicate blue flowers and strongly scented leaves.

5 A scented thyme carpet.

4 Rue flowers in summer.

6 Sage.

**1 Nasturtium**
*Tropaeolum majus*
(photograph, p. 18)

Annual, decorative plant.
**Variety:** "Alaska": yellow
and green striped. **Origin:**
Peru. **Appearance:** 40-
300 cm (16-120 in) long
shoots. Low-growing and
climbing varieties. Blue
green, shield-shaped
leaves. Brilliant yellow, red
and orange flowers from
late spring to first frosts.
**Position:** Sunny to semi-
shady. Not too nutrient-
rich soil, well drained.
**Care:** Very sensitive to
frost, do not sow out until
the middle of the last
month of spring or pre-
grow in pots. **Use:** Cress-
like, peppery taste. The
leaves and flowers give an
interesting note to salads.
The unripe, green seeds
can be pickled like
capers. Only use fresh.
**Design:** Good with
tomatoes and marigolds.
Decorative in pots.

**2 Florence fennel**
*Foeniculum vulgare dulce*
(photograph, p. 18)

Decorative, perennial
seasoning herb.
**Varieties:**
"Atropurpureum" bronze
fennel (see photograph,
p. 18). **Origin:**
Mediterranean countries.
**Appearance:** 150-
200 cm (60-80 in) tall.
Fine, feathery, fresh green
leaves. Yellow green
flower umbels in summer.

# The wide range of herbs

*Position:* Sunny. Soil containing lime, slightly moist. *Care:* Sow seed in late spring. Profusely self-sowing. *Use:* Use leaves fresh during growing season, seeds in autumn. The swollen stem base, leaves and flowers taste of sweet aniseed and go well with fish, tomatoes and cheese. Seed for making tea and to season bread. *Design:* With dahlias, roses and *Campanula*.

## 3 Rosemary
*Rosmarinus officinalis*
(photograph, p. 19)

Strongly scented, evergreen shrub, popular as a large container plant. *Origin:* Mediterranean countries. *Appearance:* 60-90 cm (24-36 in) tall. Slightly silvery, needle-like leaves. Lilac flowers, also white and pink, from early spring to early summer. *Position:* Full sunlight, will cope with semi-shade. Well-drained soil containing lime. *Care:* Overwinter in a cool, bright position if grown in a large container. Can be planted out in the garden during the summer, and will be hardy in some regions with a little winter protection. Propagation from cuttings and hanging shoots. *Use:* With lamb, potatoes, vegetables. Fresh leaves can be used any time, pick before flowering for drying. *Design:* Planted out with roses, lavender and thyme. Also in a container.

## 4 Rue
*Ruta graveolens*
(photograph, p. 19)

Hardy healing and ornamental plant with a savoury, strong scent.

*Variety:* "Jackman's Blue".
*Origin:* Mediterranean countries. *Appearance:* 30-90 cm (12-36 in) tall. Blue green, feathery leaves. Yellow flowers in early/mid summer, beautiful, angular seedheads. *Position:* Sunny, will tolerate a little shade. Well-drained soil containing lime. *Care:* Cut back vigorously in spring. Self-sowing. *Use:* For herb butter, potato soup, soft cheese. *Design:* Looks good with yellow roses or as a low-growing hedge. **Warning:** Use only small amounts. Never use during pregnancy. May cause skin allergies.

## 5 Thyme
*Thymus* spp
(photograph, p. 19)

Low-growing to prostrate semi-shrub with a strong scent.
*Species:*
● garden thyme (*T. vulgaris*)
● wild thyme (*T. serpyllum*)
● lemon thyme (*T. citriodorus*)
*Appearance:* 10-30 cm (4-12 in) tall. Narrow, small leaves, pink flowers from late spring to early autumn. *Origin:* Mediterranean countries. *Position:* Full sunlight and dry. *Care:* Easy to propagate by layering downward-hanging shoots. Replace plant after three years. Provide winter protection in regions with a rough climate. *Use:* For seasoning soups, vegetables, meat, poultry, fish. Lemon thyme can be used for sweet dishes. Leaves can be picked at any time; pick leaves for drying shortly before flowering time. Easy to dry. *Design:* As an edging around borders, under roses, for rockeries, between stone slabs and on walls.

## 6 Sage
*Salvia officinalis*
(photographs, pp. 19 and 29)

Hardy, aromatic semi-shrub.
*Varieties:*
● "Ictarine": yellow variegated
● "Purpurescens": purple red
● "Tricolor": white variegated
● "Berggarten": grey foliage
*Origin:* Mediterranean countries. *Appearance:* Soft, silvery leaves, narrow lancet-shaped to broad. Attractive light blue flowers in spring. *Position:* Sunny. Dry soil containing lime. *Care:* Winter protection in regions with a rough climate, cut back in spring. Will become very woody after three years, so make cuttings and layer downward-hanging shoots to provide for a following generation. *Use:* Spicy and strong tasting, slightly like camphor. With meats, ham, noodle dishes. *Design:* A classical companion plant for roses. Good in a herb garden and also in shrubberies.

## 7 Oregano
*Origanum vulgare*
(photograph, p. 27)

Aromatic, hardy perennial
*Varieties:*
● "Aureum": golden coloured
● "Compactum": dwarf oregano
● "Erntedank"
● "Herrenhausen" (see p. 27)
*Origin:* Southern Europe, Asia. *Appearance:* 15-50 cm (6-20 in) tall. Small, green leaves. Flower whitish or pink to lilac, from mid-summer to early autumn. *Position:* Sunny, warm. Soil containing lime. *Care:* Propagation from rhizomes. Self-sowing.

*A herb collection with lemon basil (centre) and oyster plant (front right).*

● "Minimum": low-growing
*Origin:* Sub-tropics.
*Appearance:* 20-60 cm (8-24 in) tall. Lime green or reddish, delicate leaves, flower whitish-pink. *Position:* Sunny, warm. Soil containing humus, nutrient-rich. *Care:* Do not sow outside before the end of the last month of spring, as it is sensitive to frost. Light-germinating seed so do not cover seed with soil. *Use:* With tomatoes, also in sweet dishes. Use fresh or preserve in vinegar or oil. Suitable for freezing. *Design:* Red basil livens up the vegetable garden. Attractive with *Tagetes tenuifolia* or with marigolds. Also grows well in pots.
*My tip:* Lemon basil (*O. americanum*, see photograph left) is cared for in the same way and tastes slightly of lemon.

*Use:* As a herb for pizza, with vegetables, meat, soups. Harvest before flowering, still very strong flavour after drying. *Design:* As an underplanting under fruit trees. "Aurea" with blue *Viola tricolor*.

## 8 Oyster plant
*Mertensia maritima*
(photograph above)

Hardy perennial with blue film-like appearance to leaves.
*Appearance:* 20 cm (8 in) tall. Blue flowers from mid-summer to early autumn. *Origin:* Northern Scotland, coastal plant. *Position:* Sunny to semi-shady, high humidity. Soil should not contain fresh lime.
*Care:* Protect from slugs and snails. *Use:* Leaves and stalks taste of oysters and anchovies. With salads and raw vegetables, as a garnish with salmon. Use fresh, the colour disappears when heated. *Design:* Attractive in pots beside yellow or orange flowering tagetes (*Tagetes tenuifolia*).

## 9 Basil
*Ocimum basilicum*
(photograph, p. 33)

Strongly flavoured, annual herb with many varieties.
*Varieties:*
● "Dark Opal": red leaves

## 10 Lavender
*Lavandula angustifolia*
(photograph, p. 7).

Strongly scented, decorative semi-shrub.
*Origin:* Mediterranean countries.
*Appearance:* 30-60 cm (12-24 in) tall. Silvery-grey, needle-shaped leaves. Flowers light blue to dark blue, also pink or white, during the first and second months of summer. *Position:* Full sunlight. Dry soil, containing lime. *Care:* Cut back in spring, second cut after flowering. Propagation from cuttings taken from shoots. Hardy. *Use:* Flowers for pot-pourris, scented pillows and teas. As a seasoning herb in Provençal herb mixtures, with desserts. Dry when flowering commences. *Design:* With roses, in herb gardens, as a wall plant.

*1 Sweet Cicely has a scent like aniseed.*

# Healing herbs as ornamental plants in the garden

Many of the old healing herbs from monastery gardens were so attractive that they were cultivated and crossed by gardeners and have now become firmly established in our flower gardens. Even the wild forms have a certain natural charm that will turn any herb garden into a fine display.

*2 Elecampane is a giant among perennial herbs.*

*3 A variegated comfrey variety.*

*4 Angelica has red stalks.*

*5 Marigold.*

*6 Lady's mantle has delicate flowers.*

*7 The glowing colours of bergamot.*

## 1 Sweet Cicely

*Myrrhis odorata*
(photograph, p. 22)

Strongly scented, hardy perennial.
**Origin:** Europe.
**Appearance:** 60-100 cm (24-40 in) tall. Large, feathery leaves. White flowers in the spring.
**Position:** Slightly shady. Fresh, nutrient-rich soil.
**Care:** Cut back after flowering when the plant is not intended to take up too much space. Will self-sow. **Use:** Young leaves, delicate stalks and the unripe, green seeds taste deliciously of aniseed and liquorice. Use fresh leaves, freeze seeds, dry or preserve in rum. Seeds with sweet dishes, whipped cream or ice cream. **Design:** Makes an attractive accompaniment to early-flowering perennials if underplanted with sweet woodruff (*Asperula odorata*) and forget-me-not.

## 2 Elecampane

*Inula helenium*
(photograph, p. 22)

An imposing large plant.
**Origin:** Central Asia.
**Appearance:** 150-200 cm (60-80 in) tall. Large, longish/heart-shaped, grey felted leaves. Yellow, daisy-like flowers from early summer to early autumn.
**Position:** Sunny to slightly shady. Moist, lime-rich soil.

# The wide range of herbs

*Care:* Give plenty of compost.
*Use:* The dried roots for making tea for coughs and bronchitis. Use as an aroma enhancer in pot-pourri. *Design:* A large solitary plant looks good at the back of a bed with perennials and other plants or beside a pond.

## 3 Comfrey
*Symphytum officinale*
(photograph, p. 23)

Hardy, vigorously growing perennial.
*Origin:* Central Europe.
*Appearance:* 50-100 cm (20-40 in) tall. Soft, hairy, lancet-shaped leaves, bell-shaped flowers ranging from whitish to light blue and violet, from the last month of spring to the first month of autumn. *Position:* Light semi-shade. Moist, nutrient-rich soil.
*Care:* Cut several times throughout the year. It is difficult to get rid of as the roots penetrate deep into the soil. Propagation from division. Self-sowing. *Use:* In the garden as mulch, made into fermented herbal brew and for composting.
*Design:* Along the edge of a pond, together with meadowsweet, grasses, ferns and lady's mantle. White-edged comfrey (*Symphytum grandiflorum*) "Variegatum" is very eye-catching. **Warning:** Do not use in cooking as it is suspected of causing damage to the liver.

**My tip:** Russian comfrey (*Symphytum peregrinum*) is popular as a basis for fermented herbal brews and mulching matter.

## 4 Garden angelica
*Angelica archangelica*
(photograph, p. 23)

Biennial to perennial large plant.
*Origin:* Northern, central Europe.
*Appearance:* 200-250 cm (80-100 in) tall. Light green, large, tripartite, lobed leaves. Greenish-yellow, semi-spherical umbels.
*Position:* Semi-shade. Nutrient-rich, moist soil. *Care:* Robust plant, self-sowing. *Use:* Leaves have a scent of musk. Harvest before flowering, dry or use fresh as tea. The stalks can be candied. Good with rhubarb and gooseberry jams. The root is used in perfume manufacture and in herbal liqueurs. *Design:* It is very conspicuous wherever it is planted. Good together with lady's mantle.

## 5 Marigold
*Calendula officinalis*
(photograph, p. 23)

Annual, widely dispersed.
*Origin:* Central, eastern and southern Europe, Asia.
*Appearance:* 50-70 cm (20-28 in) tall. Daisy-like, glowing yellow and orange flowers from early summer to first frosts. *Position:* Sunny. Lime-rich, slightly moist soil. *Care:* Plentifully self-sowing. If the plants are too closely placed together, infestation with aphids or mildew is likely. *Use:* Bitter, strong flavour. Use plucked out petals to add colour to meat broth, butter and cheese, rice (cheap substitute for saffron), in salads. Use in healing salves. Drying and freezing possible.
*Design:* Particularly attractive and glowing when planted with lavender (see p. 7).

## 6 Lady's mantle
*Alchemilla mollis*
(photograph, p. 23)

Attractive perennial with frothy flowers.
*Origin:* Northern Europe, Asia Minor. *Appearance:* 15-35 cm (6-14 in) tall. Velvety, hairy, "folded" leaves. Greenish-yellow flowers from early summer to late summer. *Position:* Sunny or light shade. Nutrient-rich soil. *Care:* Cut after flowering when it begins to shoot again. Profusely self-sowing. *Use:* As a decorative base for fruit and cheese. The wild form *A. xanthochtora* (syn. *A. vulgaris*) is used as a herbal tea for menopausal problems. Leaves are also placed on injuries.
*Design:* For edging beds and as ground-cover.

## 7 Bergamot
*Monarda didyma*
(photograph, p. 23)

Hardy, flavourful perennial. Hybrids are often used as ornamental plants in gardens.
*Origin:* North America.
*Appearance:* 100 cm (40 in) tall. Flowers conspicuous scarlet, pink, white or light lilac from early summer to autumn. *Position:* Sunny to semi-shady. Nutrient-rich, slightly moist soil. *Care:* Robust plant. Propagation from runners. *Use:* Flavourful leaves with a scent of lemon, fresh for herbal tea (especially good if chilled or with ice), dried as winter provisions. Flowers in salads, sweet dishes. *Design:* As a splash of colour in herb gardens. Good with grasses, day lilies, autumn asters and gypsophila.

*A sun worshipper – mullein (Verbascum densiflorum).*

### 8 Mullein
*Verbascum* spp.
(photograph above)

Biennial healing herb.
**Species:**
● *V. densiflorum*
● *V. thapsus*
**Origin:** Europe, Asia.
**Appearance:** 150-200 cm (60-80 in) tall. Prostrate rosette with large, hairy leaves. Candle-like inflorescence with light yellow, delicate flowers from the first month of summer to the first month of autumn. **Position:** Sunny. Nutrient-rich, dry soil. **Care:** Sow out in spring or summer. Self-sowing. **Use:** The flowers taste sweetish and smell of honey. Dried in teas as a cough cure, fresh in soups and salads. Only use flowers of *V. densiflorum* and *V. thapsus*. **Design:** Mullein is a dominating, ornamental plant in a herb garden and will liven up a sunny shrubbery with its long flowering period. The hybrids are popular garden plants.

### 9 Tansy
*Tanacetum balsamita*

Decorative, scented leafy perennial.
**Origin:** Far East. **Appearance:** 60-100 cm (24-40 in) tall. Green, large, oval leaves. Small, yellow flowerheads in late summer. **Position:** Full sunlight. Nutrient-rich soil, well drained. **Care:** Propagation from runners or division. **Use:** Leaves smell of mint, lemon and balm. Finely sliced very young leaves for salads and with new potatoes. Dried in pot-pourris, in laundry cupboard or airing cupboard to keep away insects. **Design:** This plant makes an attractive background for flowering herbs and low-growing roses.

### 10 Valerian
*Valeriana officinalis*

Tall, graceful, hardy perennial.
**Origin:** Europe, Asia.
**Appearance:** 100-150 cm (40-60 in) tall. Feathery leaves. Whitish-pink flowers from early summer to midsummer.
**Position:** Semi-shade. Moist soil. Will tolerate dry soil and sun.
**Care:** Robust plant, profusely self-sowing. **Use:** Dig out the roots in the autumn and dry them. Use as a tea for calming and sleep-inducing effects.
**Design:** The frothy white flowers give a romantic air to a rose garden or in shrubberies.

# Designing with herbs

Herbs can decorate any part of the garden, whether as a herb garden in the classical mould or as a decorative combination of herbs with vegetables or flowers. Here we present a host of tried and tested ideas.

*Photo above: Oregano "Herrenhausen".*
*Photo left: The author's herb garden. The delicate, candle-shaped flowers of agrimony are grouped together with comfrey, rue, and broad-leafed sage around a compact, spherical box tree.*

# Designing with herbs

## Traditional order in a herb garden

The designs of many old herb gardens indicate that herbs require certain features to bring out their beauty fully. These structures are like the "backbone" of a garden and may vary considerably.

*Architectural elements added to a garden* will endure for a long time and should, therefore, be chosen very carefully. Among these are pergolas, statues, birdbaths or troughs, paths, drystone walls and seats.

These elements should complement the house too as every garden should be seen as an extension of the house and the material and design of a house and garden should form a single unit.

On the other hand, garden structures should also blend with the general vicinity and complement the landscape. When used as structural elements, plants provide supports and form but, at the same time, can give their surroundings a natural look.

● Spherical shapes form visual centres. Even if you do not have a classical herb garden, it is still a good idea to combine herbs with spherically clipped box trees. If you cannot wait, you can also clip yews (very toxic!) or fast-growing privet into spherical shapes.

● Low hedges or borders made of box, lavender or rue may be used to edge single beds or the entire herb garden. Evergreen box is particularly attractive, although borders and edging created by parsley will save space and be just as decorative.

## Designing with different heights of growth

The different natural heights of herbs are one important factor of design which should be considered before planting anything. The plants should be arranged in such a way that you end up with a varied but harmonious finished design.

● Tall herbs, like fennel (*Foeniculum vulgare dulce*), dill (*Anethum graveolens*), angelica (*Angelica archengelica*) and lovage (*Levisticum officinale*), should be planted as a background. They also look good as solitary plants in conspicuous places.

● Medium-tall plants, like oregano (*Origanum vulgare*), sage (*Salvia officinalis*), lemon balm (*Melissa officinalis*) or mint (*Mentha* spp), constitute the main part of any planting and are very versatile in their use.

● Low-growing plants, like thyme (*Thymus vulgaris*) or parsley (*Petroselinum crispum*), will only be set off properly at the front of plantings.

## Using leaf shapes

Various different leaf shapes can also make important elements if you are intending to design with herbs. Broad leaves set beside narrow, filigree ones appear even more compact and will provide the perfect foil for the delicate beauty of flowers. For example:

● Lacy, feathery fennel leaves look even more delicate beside a compact spherical box tree.

● The shield-shaped leaves of nasturtium (*Tropaeolum majus*) planted in the foreground will contrast beautifully with delicate dill leaves.

NB: If you use herbs in garden design, you must not forget to consider the requirements, for example as to position, of the different species used (see p. 44).

## Using leaf colours

Even the colours of leaves can play an important part in design. Many herbs possess very colourful leaves that can be employed to create an effect in the same way as the colours of the flowers. In addition to the single-coloured green, grey or red species and varieties, there are also those with variegated leaves in shades of green and white or green and yellow. You will find interesting varieties of colours within the following species:

**Sage** has a particularly broad range of leaf colourings (see photograph right) which glow most vividly in spring. Coloured leaf species do not grow as vigorously as ordinary sage (*Salvia officinalis*) and will require winter protection in regions that are at risk from frosts. In addition to the varieties depicted on the right, we can also recommend the variety "Purpurescens" with its purple red leaves (see photograph, p. 33).

**Among mint plants** (*Mentha* spp) there are also many beautifully coloured leaves:
● pineapple mint (*Mentha suaveolens* "Variegata") with green and white flecked leaves
● ginger mint (*Mentha gentilis* "Variegata") with yellow markings.

*Salvia lavandulifolia.*

*Salvia officinalis "Ictarine".*

*Salvia officinalis "Tricolor".*

**My tip:** The coloured varieties do not grow as profusely as the others and can, therefore, be combined very well with perennials and annuals.

**The thyme family** (*Thymus* spp) will also enhance and bring variety to your garden with many colourful surprises:
● lemon thyme (*Thymus citriodorus* "Silver Queen") with silvery leaves
● *Thymus citriodorus* "Golden Dwarf" with yellow leaf tips.

**Lemon balm** (*Melissa officinalis*) has golden markings on its leaves. These turn green during the summer and should then be cut down.

**Comfrey** (*Symphytum officinale*) also has a colourful relative: *Symphytum grandiflorum* "Variegatum" with white-edged leaves (see photograph, p. 23).

**Basil** (*Ocimum basilicum*) provides some dark red varieties, for example the variety "Dark Opal" (see photograph, p. 33).

**Nasturtium** (*Tropaeolum majus*) also comes in a variegated form: "Alaska".

**Oregano** (*Origanum vulgare*) brings sunshine into the herb garden with the yellow-flecked variety "Aureum".

# Design

Herbs and natural stones placed together produce a harmonious effect. The soft, silvery colours of thyme, sage and lavender are very attractive with stones.

## A natural rock
(illustration 1)

Pieces of natural rock do not require a great deal of room and make ideal partners for warmth-loving herbs. Here an entire herb collection or a single lavender bush can spread out beautifully.
*Method*
● The best way to transport heavy rocks is with a wheelbarrow.
● Dig out a little soil so the rock can be sunk slightly into the ground.
● Fill the hole up with soil again.
● Plant the herbs on the south side of the rock. Maintain the usual spacing of plants.

## Drystone wall
(illustration 2)

Drystone walls are particularly suitable around a patio or for supporting a terraced garden. These are ideal places to grow thyme, lavender, rosemary, oregano and savory.

*2 A drystone wall to support a bank: Pile up natural stones on a concrete foundation and plant herbs in the cracks.*

*Method*
● Decide the course of the wall and dig a trench for the foundations.
● If the ground is firm, a depth of 20 cm (8 in) will be sufficient. The first course of stones can be placed directly on the soil.
● If the soil is fairly loose, or the wall is to attain a height of over 80 cm (32 in), you will have to lay a concrete foundation. Dig out the soil to a depth of about 40 cm (16 in) and put in a 20 cm (8 in) thick concrete foundation.

● Lay the first course of stones on the concrete before it has quite set so that they fuse together. Then leave the concrete until it is completely dry.
● Stack up the stones in such a way that the wall leans slightly towards the bank. Make sure that the cracks between the stones in one layer are bridged by the stones in the next.
● While building, place soil and plants in the cracks. Herbs that enjoy dry conditions and many other rockery and alpine plants are suitable for this site.
● A layer of gravel behind the wall will ensure that water drains away easily.
● Thyme or lady's mantle can be planted at the foot of the wall.

**My tip:** By leaving out a few stones in the top course of the wall you can create a seat that can be planted with cushion-forming plants like thyme or prostrate-growing, scented chamomile.

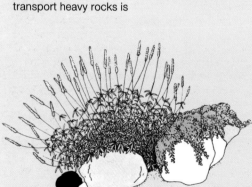

*1 Herbs with natural rocks: Lavender (back) and thyme (right) will thrive in sunny positions.*

*3 How to construct a herb spiral: Natural stones are laid in courses in the same way as in a drystone wall.*

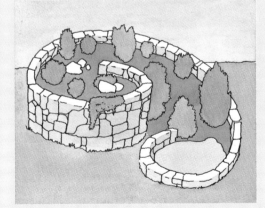

*4 How to plant in a herb spiral: The higher part of the spiral offers ideal conditions for Mediterranean herbs like sage, thyme, lavender, rosemary and marjoram. Indigenous European herbs for cooking grow in the centre. Herbs that prefer more moisture are placed directly beside the small pond in the lowest part of the spiral.*

## A herb spiral
(illustrations 3 and 4)

A herb spiral is ideal in a confined area where an entire herb community can be grown in optimal conditions. It will, however, tend to look out of place if it is built out of very large stones and should blend well with its surroundings, for example at the end of a drystone wall.

### Method
● The spiral should be built of natural stones just like a drystone wall.
● Lay out the basic outline of the spiral with a spade. Dig out about 10 cm (4 in) of soil for the first course of stones.
● Gradually build up the spiral on top of the first course of stones. The maximum height of the spiral should be about 50-60 cm (20-24 in), sloping down slightly towards the outer edge.
● Fill the space between the walls with building rubble. This material contains limestone and is water-permeable so it is ideal for herbs.
● Cover up the building rubble with a 10 cm (4 in) thick layer of soil. A mixture of two parts of garden soil and one part of sand is particularly favourable.
● The outer part of the spiral should be filled up with good garden soil.
● You could even install a small pond at the end of the herb spiral. Dig a suitable-sized hole and line it with pond liner or simply insert a large plastic bowl or tub.

### Planting
● The highest part of the spiral is the ideal place for sage, thyme, lavender, rosemary, marjoram (*Majorana hortensis*) and savory.
● The middle section can be planted with oregano, hyssop, basil, chives, parsley and salad burnet.
● Plant moisture-loving herbs in the lowest part of the spiral, like peppermint, lemon balm and watercress.

# Designing with herbs

## Herb combinations

If you are intending to plant herbs in your garden mainly with a view to using them in cooking, you will be best off with a small herb garden or herb bed. This means that all of the most frequently used herbs will be in one accessible place. If you install this herb bed near your house or patio, you will not have to walk far to harvest the herbs and will not have to plod across the entire garden in pouring rain.

**My tip:** Plant the types of herbs you use most frequently in pots on your patio or balcony. This will also save walking long distances to pick them.

## The importance of position

The requirements of different herbs with respect to position and soil are not always the same.

● The Mediterranean herbs, like rosemary, sage, thyme and lavender, love full sunlight and poor, well-drained soil.

● Most northern European herbs, on the other hand, like mint, chervil and caraway, prefer humus-rich, nutrient-rich soil in the sun or light semi-shade.

**NB:** Herbs will only develop their full scent and flavour in the correct position for their species. The exact requirements of various different herbs can be found on pages 14-25.

## Successful combinations

Here are a few well-tried ideas to copy.

### A small herb garden

A gooseberry bush underplanted with alpine strawberries can form the centre of the herb garden. Arrange four beds, separated by a cross path, to surround the centre. Permanent plants in the beds can be lemon balm, hyssop, sage, thyme, tarragon, chives and salad burnet. Every year plant fresh parsley, chervil and basil. Borage and marigolds will self-sow once they have been planted or sown. If you have room for a larger herb garden, you can integrate rarer herbs like rue, agrimony, and *Tanacetum balsamita* for their ornamental qualities.

### A sunshine-yellow herb bed

Designing according to colours can look very attractive and harmonious. Try a sunny yellow herb bed, for example. Yellow-flowering herbs like St. John's wort, yarrow, agrimony, rue, stonecrop (*Sedum reflexum*) or fennel can be complemented with varieties with yellow-green foliage, for example *Salvia officinalis* "Ictarine", *Origanum vulgare* "Aureum", *Melissa officinalis* "Aurea" or *Thymus citriodorus* "Golden Dwarf".

If you add continuous-flowering marigolds whose glowing colours never fade all summer long, you will have your own sunshine even on dull days!

### Mediterranean herb bed

This is the place for different species of sage (see p. 29). Lavender looks good beside the silvery leaves of *Salvia officinalis* "Berggarten". A collection of different thyme species will set this off. Blue and white iris (*Iris sibirica*) make an attractive accompaniment.

### Herbs for edging

Some herbs can be formed into low-growing hedges and used to edge entire beds. Particularly suitable are lavender (*Lavandula angustifolia*), rue (*Ruta graveolens*), especially the compact variety "Jackman's Blue" (see inside front cover) and thyme (*Thymus vulgaris*). The low-growing form of oregano (*Origanum vulgare* "Compactum") and rue can also be used as an edging for a central roundel.

The purple leaves of Salvia officinalis "Purpurescens" make a contrast to other herbs in varying shades of green.

Basil "Dark Opal".

**My tip:** As larger quantities of herbs are required for hedges, it is a good idea to propagate them yourself: from cuttings (lavender), by sowing (rue, thyme) or by layering (oregano, thyme).

**Special places for herbs**

Comfrey (*Symphytum officinale*) and horse radish (*Armoracia rusticana*) are extremely invasive and their desire to spread is hard to cope with. They are very decorative in regard to both leaves and flowers, so do plant them but make sure to isolate them. Placed around a pond or under fruit trees, they will not get in the way of less vigorously growing plants.

33

# Designing with herbs

## Herbs and vegetables

The foliage of many species of vegetables is as decorative as flowers: red cabbage with its purple red leaves, crinkly lettuces in all their different varieties, blue dwarf beans, glowing yellow courgettes and ruby red mangel-wurzel. Both historical and modern examples of enchanting kitchen gardens prove that colourful flowers and herbs go extremely well with vegetables. In particular, the annual and biennial herbs used for cooking, like dill, chervil, parsley, caraway, coriander and basil, go well with lettuces and other vegetables. Just like the vegetables, they require nutrient-rich soil to develop fully throughout one season.
**NB:** Alternate your crops. Herbs like parsley or dill should not be planted in the same place several years running. In addition, the plants should be well spaced out so that they do not jostle each other for room.

## Colourful beds all year round

Try these attractive combinations for the vegetable garden:
● Salad burnet goes extremely well with red iceberg lettuce "Red Sioux".
● The delicate leaves of chervil tower gracefully above the lettuce variety "Lollo Rosso".
● Colourful lettuce combinations are decorative with radishes, cress, hedge mustard (*Sisymbrium officinale*), basil and chives.
● Lettuces and annual herbs make ideal partners. Mix the seeds and sow them generously over a large area. Harvest the seedlings for mixed salad, cutting them when they are 5-10 cm (2-4 in) tall. At this stage of growth they contain more vitamins and minerals than when they are fully grown. Leave some plants standing so that they can develop into fully grown lettuce heads.

**My tip:** If you sow several batches of seed at intervals of two to three weeks, you will be able to harvest lettuces throughout the entire season. A late sowing in autumn may even overwinter.

## Winter bed with herbs
Even in winter, a vegetable bed need not be bare. Try planting a winter bed with lamb's lettuce and herbs that are sown in alternating rows. Quite a number of herbs are hardy and very suitable for this method, such as salad burnet, chervil, *Portulaca oleracea*, rue, parsley and yellow rocket (*Barbarea vulgaris*).

## Varied uses

A combination of herbs with vegetables is not only decorative but useful in many different ways.
● Scented herbs attract honeybees and bumble bees which are responsible for pollinating fruit and vegetables, for example tomatoes and courgettes.
● A herb and shrub "shield" around the vegetables will keep slugs, snails and other pests out. Chervil, in particular, protects lettuces from slugs and snails. It is also a good neighbour for all plants that are susceptible to mildew.
● Ants very much dislike herbs such as lavender, marigolds, crinkly mint and chives.
● Some plants protect themselves, and their neighbours, against pests and diseases with secretions from their leaves and roots. Vigorous growth and flavour can also be enhanced by the presence of favourable neighbouring plants. Mildew and other fungal infections occur less often and the plants are healthier.

## Useful partnerships include:
● tomatoes with parsley, nasturtium and basil
● beetroot with coriander, savory, dill and basil
● lettuces with chervil, *Portulaca*, basil and chives.

## Unfavourable combinations include:

● bergamot (*Monarda*) beside lemon balm
● parsley beside lettuce
● lovage and wormwood are said to have a growth-restricting effect on other plants.

## Herbs for fertilizing and pest control

You can use herbs in any garden as cost-free fertilizer and pest control.

*Herbs made into mulch* keep the garden healthy. Vigorously growing plants, like comfrey, can be cut down several times a year and used as mulch between rows of vegetables, around tree roots or under roses. Compost can also be enriched with the leaves.

*Growth-promoting, fermented herbal brews* can be employed throughout the summer instead of mineral fertilizers. When using a medium amount of organic fertilizer, the levels of nitrates that result in vegetables and lettuces will be lower than if you use mineral fertilizers. Nevertheless, you should be sparing with organic fertilizers such as compost and fermented herbal brews.

*Herbal teas* can be used as a preventive or as a targeted treatment for the control of pests.

## Herb combinations for fermented brews and sprays

### Fermented brews

● Fermented comfrey brew is particularly good for vegetables with fruits (e.g. tomatoes).
● Fermented fennel brew encourages growth.
● Fermented marigold brew fortifies plants.
● A fermented herbal brew made of sage, thyme, lovage, lavender, mint and mugwort (*Artemisia vulgaris*) strengthens the resistance of plants to all kinds of disease.

*Method*
● Place the cut leaves in a plastic or pottery vessel and fill this with about 10 litres (17½ pt) fresh water to every 1 kg (2¼ lb) of fresh leaves.
● Stir well once or twice a day to add oxygen.
● The mixture should begin to ferment after about 10-14 days.
● Once the brew has stopped producing gas bubbles, the process is complete and the liquid can be used after straining. Fermented brews should be diluted with water in the ratio 1:5 to 1:10 to avoid leaf burns on the plants being watered.
● When you have removed the brew, you can use the remaining plant matter as mulch around vegetable plants.

### Sprays

*Horseradish spray:* Add 500 g (1 lb) leaves and grated roots to 1 litre (1¾ pt) water. *Application:* Spray undiluted on to fruit trees using a plant spray device at blossom time. *Effect:* Protection against various pests and diseases.

*Wormwood spray:* Add 150 g (5¼ oz) wormwood leaves and flowers to 5 litres (8¾ pt) water. *Application:* To control aphids and insect larvae during early and midsummer; dilute 1:3 in water and spray affected plants. Use in a targeted, sparing manner. *Effect:* Wormwood has a caustic effect and will kill pests.

*Mixed herb spray:* Garlic, horseradish, yarrow and chamomile (20 g or ½ oz to 2 litres or 3½ pt water). *Application:* for all plants that are susceptible to infestation with mildew and rust. Spray the soil and leaves every two weeks as a preventive. *Effect:* Kills germs. Destroys fungi and bacteria.

*Method*
Pour boiling water over the leaves just like when making tea. Allow to draw for 20 minutes and strain.

# Designing with herbs

## Herbs and roses

Romantic garden scenes can be created when herbs are combined with roses. They were once frequently planted together in monastery gardens in order to enhance each other's charm. Watch the following points, however:

● Be sparing with fertilizer for the roses or the herbs will grow too vigorously.

● Regular cutting back in the spring will preserve the shape of the herbs and the roses will not be overrun.

## Classical company for roses

Among the best companion plants are sage, thyme and lavender as their etheric oils will keep pests at bay.

*Sage* (*Salvia*) offers many variations of colourful leaves which can form a pretty ring around the roses.

● The grey-leafed variety "Berggarten", with its particularly large, soft leaves, makes a very decorative underplanting.

● The variety *Salvia lavandulifolia*, which smells faintly of lavender, is often chosen for its particularly beautiful flowers in spring.

● The biennial muscatel sage (*Salvia sclarea*) lends a particularly romantic air and its striking flowers provide a beautiful bed for months. The shimmering pink to light lilac outer petals fade in a very decorative manner. They can be plucked off in late summer and used for a strongly scented pot-pourri (see p. 57).

*Thyme* (*Thymus*): All species and varieties are suitable as scented carpet plants at the base of bush roses in sunny positions.

*Lavender* (*Lavandula angustifolia*) goes very well with white, pink and red floribunda roses and with low-growing white bush roses growing in full sunlight.

## Attractive, unusual neighbours

Many other herbs can also make charming partners for roses. Try some of the following combinations:

*Chives* (*Allium schoenoprasum*): The pink flowers go surprisingly well with roses in cool shades of pink, for example, "Centennaire de Lourdes".

*Rue* (*Ruta graveolens*): You can create particularly decorative effects with this plant, for example when combined with the English rose "Yellow Charles Austin", when the fruity, lemony scent of the rose combines well with the spicy scent of rue. The two plants also look good together in a vase. The angular, greenish-yellow seedheads of rue, which form in late summer, also complement the roses. Yellow-flowering St. John's wort (*Hypericum* species) is another plant that goes well with rue.

*Fennel* (*Foeniculum vulgare*) is an excellent partner for roses. Planted together with yellow bush roses, its delicate, frothy umbels tone down colours that are too strong and help them to blend with the colours of other roses.

*Bronze fennel* (*Foeniculum vulgare* "Atropurpurea") looks ravishing with the white bush rose "Schneewittchen".

*Wormwood and rue* (*Artemisia absinthium* and *A. abrotanum*): Their delicate, silvery, shimmering foliage is particularly attractive with white roses. If you want an entire bed of white flowers, you can grow these with white lilies, iris and woundwort (*Stachys byzantina*). In the spring, you could have white pansies, white narcissus and white tulips.

*Bush rose "Golden Showers" underplanted with a small herb garden including tarragon, rue, Sedum reflexum and pinkish-violet flowering chives.*

# Designing with herbs

Gypsophila, valerian and a silver white standard rose pruned into a spherical shape will produce a most elegant effect in the summer.

**Valerian** (*Valeriana officinalis*) insinuates itself around roses in a very attractive, romantic manner. Its tiny white flowers make it look almost like giant gypsophila. Its scent is not regarded as pleasant by all humans, however, although it is very popular with cats.

**Tanacetum balsamita** also makes an attractive partner for roses. If you combine it with the vigorous "Gloria Dei" and delicate blue lavender, you will have all the classic herbs and flowers for scenting your laundry combined in one place.

## Herbs in a flower garden

Lovely plant groupings can be created with herbs in a flower garden.

**Vigorous colour contrasts** can be obtained with the following combinations:
- marigolds (*Calendula officinalis*) with red basil (*Ocimum basilicum* "Dark Opal")
- pansies (*Viola tricolor*) with golden oregano (*Origanum vulgare* "Aureum") and chives (*Allium schoenoprasum*)
- yellow and red gladioli with nasturtiums (*Tropaeolum majus*)

- bergamot (*Monarda didyma*) with rue (*Ruta graveolens*)
- marigolds (*Calendula officinalis*) with lavender (*Lavandula angustifolia*) (see p. 7)
- pink, red and white lupins (*Lupinus* hybrids) with sage (*Salvia officinalis*)

**Rather more delicate combinations include:**
- borage (*Borago officinalis*) in front of *Hosta sieboldiana* "Elegans"
- thyme (*Thymus vulgaris*) and regal lily (*Lilium regale*)
- *Campanula* species with ginger mint (*Mentha gentilis*)
- paeonies (*Paeonia* species and hybrids) and sage (*Salvia officinalis*)

Herbs with interesting leaves in soft shades of green provide a quiet background for colourful stands of perennials.
- *Myrrhis odorata*, with its white umbels smelling of aniseed, is attractive in spring plantings together with tulips, narcissi and forget-me-not (*Myosotis*). When it spreads its feathery leaves in the summer, it is able to cover up the unattractive yellowing leaves of the bulbous plants.
- Lady's mantle (*Alchemilla mollis*) has attractive leaves and flowers and is often regarded as an ornamental plant rather than a herb. It seems to heighten the intensity of colours in a shrubbery and adds a fresh look. Lady's mantle can be

employed anywhere: with shrubs, with roses and, of course, with other herbs.
- *Tanacetum balsamita* has lime green leaves that smell strongly of mint, lemon and balm. It provides an attractive background for low-growing perennials. Try planting *Tanacetum balsamita* with *Campanula* or *Geranium* species. *Tanacetum* was often used as a book mark in hymnbooks once upon a time. Its refreshing scent is released on touch. If it is planted close to a much frequented path, you can pick off the occasional leaf to sniff at.

**My tip:** Herbs in your shrubbery and flowerbeds make weeding a pleasant chore. When pulling up weeds you will brush against the herbs and release the wonderful scents of mint, fresh lemon or orange from plants like mint, lemon balm and bergamot (*Monarda*).

*A cheerful summer planting including the pink flowers of chives, spignel (Meum anthamanticum) and blue and white irises.*

## Flowering kitchen herbs

Years ago, there was a tendency to hide chives (*Allium schoenoprasum*) and parsley (*Petroselinum crispum*) in the vegetable patch but now they have been rediscovered for use in flowerbeds.

If, however, you follow the often-quoted advice to cut off the flowerheads of chives before they open, you will never have an opportunity to discover how very attractive these spherical pink flowers really are. They can be combined not only with roses but also with many handsome species of *Iris*. In spite of the fact that parsley is probably the most common of all herbs used in the kitchen, you rarely see it in a flowergarden. Its crinkly leaves give it a lacy, old-fashioned charm. Grow it with scented pelargoniums and pansies (*Viola tricolor*) to form a very harmonious trio. Smooth-leafed parsley has a stronger taste but is not quite so decorative.

# Designing with herbs

*A lavender path leading to a secluded garden seat.*

*Herb steps planted with lady's mantle.*

## Further designing tips

***Herbs planted in cracks:***
Cracks between the stone slabs of a footpath are ideal for planting with herbs. Thyme species, in particular, seem quite happy with the rather spartan conditions in these positions, for example lemon thyme (*Thymus citriodoros*) or wild thyme (*Thymus serpyllum*). Clouds of aromatic scent are released when they are trodden on.

***A herb stair:*** Steps planted with thyme, which lead up to a sunny patio, combine the practical with the beautiful as you will find when you sit on the steps to enjoy the warm scent and daydream a little on sunny days. Steps planted with delicate lady's mantle (*Alchemilla mollis*) are also most attractive.

**NB:** Always consider the position when planting in this way. Thyme species must be given a position in full sunlight. Lady's mantle, on the other hand, prefers a semi-shady location.

***Herbs in a raised bed:*** A raised bed edged with stones provides the right conditions for herbs and will save you a lot of bending down during care and harvesting. Plant low-growing, overhanging herbs like rosemary (*Rosmarinus repens*) or stonecrop (*Sedum reflexum*) around the edge.

## Herbs in a pot

Nearly all herbs will grow quite happily in pots, boxes and troughs or other large containers.

● Bay and rosemary are classic large container plants. These natives of southern regions are sensitive to frost and will survive the winter best if placed in a cool, bright position in the house or conservatory. If they are not planted out in the garden, but kept in a large container, they will be easier to bring inside for the winter.

● Sage, rosemary, savory and thyme grow happily in poor, stony soil. They feel quite at home in pots and will not mind too much if you occasionally forget to water them. They will thrive in a mixture of soil and sand (3:1) and require a position in full sunlight.

● Annual and biennial kitchen herbs, like basil, chervil, chives and parsley, require good, humus-rich soil. They have to be watered regularly and fertilized every two to four weeks. Summer savory, oregano, lemon balm and salad burnet require nutritious soil and regular care.

*Positions:* The most frequently used positions for herbs in pots are patios and balconies. Try planting robust herbs instead of the usual balcony plants. Summer flowers grouped with herbs will make a pleasing picture. You can try out new combinations every year. Also try positioning the pots in three different dimensions in order to utilize the available space: for example, on the ground, on walls, on steps and on tables and also in hanging baskets on the wall.

You can create visual interest in the garden as well by using herbs in pots. For example, seasonal gaps in beds can be filled in a most attractive way with herbs in containers and pots.

### Planting combinations

● Violet heliotrope, with its wonderful scent of vanilla, goes well with sage, thyme and lavender.

● The large mint family is eminently suitable for semi-shady positions, together with wood sorrel (*Oxalis acetosella*), parsley and chives.

● Cherry tomatoes in a pot or balcony box go well with basil, parsley, garlic or glowing yellow or orange nasturtiums.

● Silvery wormwood looks very good with white pansies.

## Conspicuous herbs as solitary plants

Large, bushy herbs will create an eye-catching feature if they are planted singly in a good position. Given plenty of nutrition and a suitable site, these striking plants can grow up to 1•8 m (6 ft) tall. Lower shrubs can be added around them although the main plant will always command most attention.

● Fennel (*Foeniculum vulgare*) grows so tall that it can be planned in from the start as part of a visual screen. A fully grown clump of fennel may grow taller than an adult person in the summer!

● Mullein (*Verbascum* species) rapidly sows itself. Sometimes the plants seem to choose quite decorative positions but, in any case, excessive numbers of seedlings are easily removed.

● Elecampane (*Inula helenium*) is best planted in the background of a shrubbery. Marigolds planted along the edge of the bed will echo both the shape and the colours.

● Angelica (*Angelica archangelica*), with its fresh green leaves, looks particularlay good near a pond.

# Growing herbs

Herbs will only look attractive and develop their full scent and health-giving qualities if all of their requirements as to the right living conditions are met. In particular, this means the right conditions with respect to light, temperature and soil. Our notes on care should help you to avoid any disappointments.

*Photo above: Nasturtium flower.*
*Photo left: Kitchen herbs in pots.*

# Growing herbs

## Choosing herbs

There is a huge range of herbs for sale. For beginners, in particular, this can present difficulties when making choices. My advice is to start out with a small basic stock of herbs. This ensures that you can still keep track of your selection and will enable you to expand the following year as you gather experience. Consider the following important points when making your choices.

*Use:* What uses are most important to you:
● herbs for cooking
● herbs for healing teas
● herbs as scented plants
● herbs as ornamental plants.

You will find information and details on individual herbs in the plant descriptions on pages 14-25 and in the recipe suggestions on pages 56-7.

*Function:* Do you wish to plant the herbs together with other plants or to keep them in a special bed all by themselves? If you intend to fill a gap in a flowerbed with a herb, you will need to consider the available light and soil and will only be able to choose herbs that will grow well in that particular position.

*Position:* Light and warmth are essential for most herbs. Think about the positions you can offer your herbs before purchasing them. Soil conditions are also important. Some herbs will thrive on humus-rich soil; others prefer poor, lime-rich soil. Special soil conditions can be artificially created in a herb bed or in a herb spiral (see p. 31).

## Sun or shade

Very roughly speaking, herbs can be divided up into three groups:
● Herbs for a position with full sunlight. They will require plenty of warmth and about seven hours of sunlight per day to develop their full aroma. Their typical small, narrow, tough leaves cut down on loss of water through evaporation. This means that they are optimally adapted to the dry climatic conditions of their native environments. Among these are lavender, oregano, rosemary and thyme.
● Herbs for semi-shady positions require only about four hours of sunlight per day. Among these are lemon balm, bergamot (*Monarda*), mint, parsley, chervil and salad burnet, all of which have delicate, soft leaves which do not protect the plants against evaporation.
● The conspicuous, white or yellow variegated leaves of some varieties like alternating sunlight and shade. Intense sunlight will make the edges of the leaves go brown very quickly and the glowing colours will fade. Too much shade, on the other hand, will turn the leaves completely green.

## Soil

In addition to sun and light, herbs will also need to find the right nutrients in their soil if they are to grow strong and healthy so that you can harvest perfect plants. The quality of the essential oils contained in the plants will also be determined by the soil and fertilizer.

Herbs can be roughly divided into two categories according to their requirements.

*Herbs that love humus-rich, loose soils:* The soil should not, however, contain too many nutrients or the plants will rapidly grow lots of leaves and the aroma and flavour will suffer.

*Herbs that love poorer, lime-rich soils:* These are mainly the Mediterranean herbs like rosemary, lavender and sage.

**NB:** The exact soil requirements of individual herbs can be found in the brief descriptions on pages 14-25.

*Oregano, sage, yarrow and lavender thrive in a warm, sunny position.*

## Protection from wind

Another important factor is protection from wind. For this reason, plant them where they are protected by walls or near the house or garage. Taller plants, like box or yew (very toxic!), may serve as protection. Low-growing box hedges around herb beds not only look good, they also improve the mini-climate.

**My tip:** Carry a "herb notebook" whenever you take a walk around the garden. Note down any particular observations about the plants. In this way you will be able to record both mistakes and successes, which will be a great help when planning for the following year in the garden.

*Butterflies love oregano flowers.*

# Propagating

A basic distinction is made between generative propagation (sowing seed) and vegetative propagation (from cuttings, layering downward-hanging shoots, division).

## Sowing seed

**_Annual and biennial herbs_** are easy to sow.

● Parsley, cress and chervil are not too sensitive to cold and can be sown out as early as the first month of spring. Always delay sowing until the soil has warmed up as this will help the seed to germinate faster.

● Summer savory, aniseed and coriander can be sown outside from the second and third months of spring onwards.

● Herbs that are sensitive to frost, like basil, marjoram and nasturtium, should be pre-grown on a bright windowsill or in a greenhouse. The pricked out seedlings can then be planted out in the right positions towards the end of spring.

**_Perennial herbs_** are best bought as individual plants as one

*2 Cuttings*
*a Plant cuttings in a pot and water well.*
*b A plastic bag over crossed wires creates humidity.*

plant is generally sufficient for the requirements of one household. In the case of thyme, however, sowing is also recommended as it germinates very easily and you will then have a number of small plants at your disposal.

**_Method_**

● The compost used for growing herbs should be fairly poor. You can obtain special growing mediums in the gardening trade, which have to be mixed with extra sand for use with herbs.

● Fill seed trays, pots or mini-propagators with compost.

● Sprinkle the seed very sparingly on to the compost. The closer together the seeds fall,

the less well the seedlings will develop. Exceptions are chervil and chives which should be sown densely.

● Make a note of which herbs are light-germinating (for example, marjoram, savory and basil). These seeds will only germinate in light conditions so press the seed down gently into the compost but do not cover them. Dark-germinating seed should be covered with a thin layer of soil or compost to a thickness of about three times the length of the seed.

● Moisten the compost after sowing, using a spray bottle.

● Keep the compost moist until the seedlings appear.

*1 **Nasturtium** has colourful flowers and large seeds that are easy to sow.*

### Self-sowing herbs

If you do not cut back faded shoots, fennel, borage, marigolds, wormwood, lemon balm, valerian, angelica, chives and oregano will sow themselves. The seedlings need only be thinned out a little or replanted in a better position. If you do not want any plants the following year, cut back the herbs when they start to flower.

**My tip:** Do not do a great deal of weeding in a herb garden! In the spring, wait to see if any seedlings appear before tilling the soil.

### Propagation from cuttings
(illustration 2)

Cuttings of sage, lavender and rosemary will quickly take root.
*Method*
● Cut off a shoot tip measuring about 5-8 cm (2-3 in).
● Remove the lower leaves. Allow four to five leaves to remain at the tip.
● Set the shoot tip cuttings around the edges of a pot of compost or in a mixture of sand and compost (see illustration 2a).
● Seal off the pot inside a transparent plastic bag. The cuttings will form roots better in a very humid atmosphere (see illustration 2b).
● Remove the plastic

bag when the first new shoots appear. Water regularly.
● Plant the rooted cuttings in the garden in early autumn. Overwinter rosemary inside the house.

*4 Dividing: Pull the rootstock apart.*

### Propagating by layering downward-hanging shoots
(illustration 3)

Layering downward-hanging shoots is one of the simplest ways to propagate and one that even beginners should be successful with. Long trailing shoots of thyme, lavender, hyssop and sage will often root themselves in the soil. After a while, when the shoot has developed good roots, the new young plant

can be separated from the parent plant and positioned somewhere else.

You can help with this process if you press down a long shoot into the soil and heap up a little soil around it to encourage rooting. If a very tough shoot is to be kept in this position, use a piece of wire, bent into a U shape, to pin the shoot to the soil (see illustration 3).

### Dividing a root
(illustration 4)

Root division is particularly easy for mint, tarragon, elecampane and comfrey. During the course of many years these plants produce great clumps which can be rejuvenated by division. Use a garden fork to split the clump in half sometime in the autumn or spring, lift one half out of the soil and plant it in a different position.

*3 Use a bent piece of wire to anchor a downward-hanging shoot to the soil. Cover with a little soil.*

# Growing herbs

The yellowish-green umbels of angelica (Angelica archangelica) rise above the varied green of the herbs. As can be seen here, angelica is very conspicuous in appearance and is also particularly suited for use as a solitary plant.

## Buying herbs

Some of the most popular herbs are now offered for sale pre-grown in pots in many garden centres and nurseries. You will only be able to obtain the less well-known herbs and rarities from specialist mail order firms or perhaps from other gardeners or herb-growers. The plants should look healthy and have plenty of roots.

## Planting herbs

Spring and autumn are the best times for planting. Container plants can always be planted out provided it is not too cold and not too dry. The ideal day for planting is a warm but overcast day. If the soil is too dry, it should be well watered before planting.
● Water the herbs well before planting so that the rootstock can soak itself full of water.
● Dig large enough planting holes.
● Carefully remove herbs from their pots. Loosen the rootstock slightly and set the plant a little deeper in the soil than it was in its pot.
● Fill the hole all round with soil, press down and water well.

## Jobs for the spring

● Plants that are sensitive to frost and that were covered up all winter should now have their winter protection removed.
● As soon as the soil is fairly dry, it should be carefully loosened without damaging the roots of the plants. A three-tined rake is best suited to this job.
● Spring is the optimal time for fertilizing. The ideal fertilizer for herbs is ripe compost. Sprinkle a thin layer on top of the soil and rake it in superficially. An additional handful of hoof and horn fertilizer is only necessary for herbs with a high nutrient demand, like lovage, angelica, chives and horseradish.
**NB:** Herbs do not like fresh manure!
● Shorten some of the lateral shoots to about a hand's width above the ground for large, bushy herbs like fennel and lovage. This will cut down on the space required.
● Low-growing herbs, like lavender, thyme, sage and hyssop, will cope with a gentle pruning in spring. Do not cut lavender right back into the old wood as it will then not produce new shoots (other herbs will not mind so much).

## Jobs for the summer

● Regular harvesting will retain the shape of the herbs which, otherwise, would soon look tired and straggly. Lemon balm, mint, thyme, sage and hyssop should be cut back regularly to ensure that they remain bushy. Shortening the shoot tips of basil will encourage the plants to branch out.
● Most herbs will manage without watering over longish periods of dry weather. Regular watering is very important, on the other hand, for herbs grown in pots.
● You can propagate all summer long by layering the downward-hanging shoots of lavender, savory, thyme, sage and rosemary (see p. 47).

## Jobs for the autumn

*Annual herbs* like basil and dill will die off after the first frost. *Perennial herbs* can, as a rule, overwinter outside.
● Herbs that are sensitive to frost, for example rosemary, can be covered with straw, dead bracken or conifer branches. In regions where the climate is rough, it is a good idea to overwinter them in large containers in a bright, unheated, frost-free position indoors.

# Growing herbs

● Hardy herbs, like parsley, chervil, salad burnet and hedge mustard, are impervious to the cold and will even carry on growing in frost-free periods. You can harvest a few leaves of these, along with leaves of rue, sage and thyme.

## Overwintering in a pot

If you transfer individual herbs to pots in the autumn and take them into the house for overwintering, you will be able to use herbs all year round. Basil, parsley and even mint and chives will enhance your menu in winter.

● Dig out clumps of chives and allow them to lie outside until the first frost. They require a touch of frost before they will start shooting again in a pot.

● Rosemary and bay can remain outside in pots until the first month of winter. If they are kept close to the house they will even cope with temperatures around freezing. Only if the frost is more severe should they be brought into the house. Stand them outside again during mild periods. This will help them through the winter.

● When planting the herbs in pots, make sure that the pots are large enough.

● Herbs in the house need a bright window position, as well as high humidity. Supply them with water regularly and mist frequently. Avoid too much watering.

**My tip:** Fill a large dish with Hortag and stand the herbs in pots close together in the dish. This mini-climate is better for a group of plants.

## Pests and diseases

Herbs possess their own form of protection against insects. Etheric oils in the flowers and leaves have a deterrent effect on many harmful insects. Most pests will also avoid leaves thickly covered with hairs, for example borage. This means that most herbs are not much troubled by insects.

The basic way to ensure good health is to give the plants a position with optimal conditions (see p. 44).

## Be alert when purchasing herbs

Newly bought herbs can be a means of entry by pests to your garden. Check plants carefully before buying them, particularly the undersides of leaves which is where pests like thrips, white fly, spider mites and scale insects love to hide. Discoloration of the leaves may also be an indicator of infestation with pests. If you notice an infestation after you

have bought the plant, bathing the plant in a soap solution may often help. Stand the pot in a plastic bag and tie the bag up at the rim to hold the compost in place. Fill a bucket with lukewarm water and add a few squirts of liquid soap. Immerse the plant upside down in the bucket and carefully rinse off the pests. Rinse thoroughly with clear water afterwards. Repeat the procedure the following day. If the infestation is too severe, it is better to destroy the plant. Chemical plant protection agents should be absolutely taboo in a herb garden if the herbs are intended for human consumption and if you require the help of insects and bees in pollination.

## Helpers in controlling pests

Both pests and useful insects have their place in the natural cycle of life. When pests start to get the upperhand though, they begin to represent a risk to garden plants. Usually, however, useful insects which prey on pests can be found alongside them.

*Etheric oils and leaves covered in fine hairs protect herbs from insects.*

# Growing herbs

**Ladybirds** are useful helpers in the battle against aphids. Wormwood, nasturtiums and borage are often infested with aphids. Try planting a clump of yarrow and allow the dried heads to remain in the bed as winter quarters for the ladybirds.

**Lacewings** and hover flies, whose larvae prey on aphids, live on pollen and nectar. Seed mixtures of flowers that attract these useful insects can be purchased and these plants will provide food and overwintering quarters for the insects. Do not remove the withered parts of the plants until the following spring.

## Common diseases and pests

**Rust** may appear on mint if the plants are placed too close together. Thinning out is the best help for this problem. Cut the plants down to ground level; they will shoot again in the spring.

**Mildew** may appear on borage if the plants are growing too close together. Here, too, thinning out and cutting back will help. If necessary, resow in a different position.

**Slugs and snails** can attain plague-like proportions during a wet summer. They love basil above all plants but will also attack oyster plants.

### How to control slugs and snails

● Surround the herbs with protective plants, for example cuttings of sage and lavender, chervil plants, onion sets and thyme as an edging around the bed.

● Dust the plants with a biological preparation. Consult your garden centre and buy one that will also keep off aphids and turnip flea beetles (*Phyllotreta nemorum*) and thus help the plants to grow vigorously. Repeat the procedure after rain.

● Lay borage as mulching material around the endangered herbs. Slugs and snails do not like hairy leaves.

● Collecting slugs and snails during the evening hours is a very effective measure. You can also go on night-time foraging expeditions, equipped with a torch.

**My tip:** Do not use slug pellets as many useful insects will also be destroyed by them.

## Harvesting herbs

Regular harvesting throughout the entire summer is very important for many herbs as cutting back keeps the herbs in shape.

**Cut close to the ground:** lemon balm, mint and tarragon.

**Cut the shoot tips** of rosemary, thyme and sage.

This can be done on a regular basis throughout the season. It will also encourage bushy growth and prevent the herbs from growing straggly.

**The right moment to harvest** Most herbs should be harvested shortly before flowering. The exceptions are herbs like lavender or caraway whose flowers or seeds are used. The best time is late morning on sunny days as soon as the morning dew has dried.

## Preserving herbs

**Drying:** The simplest way to preserve herbs is still the classic method of drying in the air. To do this, just bundle the stalks together and hang the bunches in a not too bright, but warm and airy place. Ideal places are a hallway inside the house, the attic and the cellar. As soon as the herbs are so dry that they rustle when touched, the leaves should be removed from the stalks and kept in opaque, screw-top containers until they are needed. If possible, do not keep herbs for longer than one year, that is only from one harvest to the next.

If you decide to dry them in the oven or in a drier, make sure that the temperature never exceeds 35°C (95°F). If too much heat is generated, the etheric oils will evaporate.

*You can enjoy the scent of herbs from a garden seat placed right among them.*

**Freezing:** The following herbs are particularly suited to this process: basil, dill, parsley and chives for cooking; mint and lemon balm for teas.

**Pickling in oil and salt**

Basil and other herbs like chives and parsley are suitable for making herb seasoning pastes. Chopped very finely and mixed with oil and salt, they will keep for several months in a screwtop jar. The herbs should always be entirely covered in oil so that they cannot turn mouldy. Reckon on 100 g (3½ oz) herbs to 1 teaspoon salt. Herbs preserved in this way are very suitable for seasoning pesto sauce, salad dressings and soups.

**Pickling in vinegar or oil:**

Vinegar and oil can be aromatically enhanced with herbs. The following recipes require ½ litre (¾ pt) vinegar/oil:
● wine vinegar with basil and one or two cloves of garlic
● vinegar essence (diluted) with a sprig of tarragon
● olive oil with one sprig each of rosemary, sage, thyme and one or two cloves of garlic
● sunflower oil with three or four bay leaves and 2 teaspoons coriander.

# Using herbs

*Vinegar with nasturtium flowers for seasoning salads.*

*A creamy potato soup served with herbs and edible flowers.*

## Uses of herbs

*Herbs can be be used in many different ways in cooking:*
- as salad herbs
- for seasoning meat, fish and vegetables
- for adding flavour to vinegar and oil
- for seasoning quark and butter
- for decorating savoury dishes and desserts

*Herbs are indispensable for health and well-being:* fresh to take full advantage of their content of vitamins and minerals; dried as herbal teas or in soothing baths for their many healing properties.

*As a decoration*, use fresh or dried herbs as a colourful display in a vase, as a table decoration or in a pot-pourri.

## Herbs in cooking

*All salads* are enhanced by the aromas and delicious flavours of herbs, not to mention the vitamins and minerals contained in them.
- Mint and lemon balm should be chopped finely or whole leaves can be mixed into the salad.
- Salad burnet can also be used as whole leaves or chopped.
- Chervil leaves in a salad give it a wonderful flavour.

● The oyster plant (see p. 21) has soft bluish leaves that will make any salad look almost exotic. It is quite a delicacy when served as a garnish with strips of smoked salmon as an hors-d'oeuvre before a special meal.

● The cress-like taste of rue is delicious in salads and sauces. Harvest very young leaves!

**Tomatoes** are a very good base for trying out the whole range of herbs one by one. Simply slice up tomatoes, arrange them in a circle on a plate and sprinkle chopped herbs over them. The following herbs are recommended: basil, tarragon, Florence fennel, oregano and savory. An additional enhancement is obtained with the use of coarsely ground sea salt and black pepper (best done in a mortar).

**Herb butter** will be particularly tasty with a mixture of fresh garden herbs. Try a mixture of herbs containing plenty of salad burnet, chives and parsley, also a little rue, sage, tarragon, hyssop and lemon thyme. Wash the herbs, dry them and chop them medium finely. Knead them into room-temperature-soft butter with added sea salt amd black pepper. Herb butter is good for freezing and will go extremely well with baguettes or lightly fried meats.

## Important rules for the use of herbs

● Only use the herbs and flowers that you know very well.

● The substances contained in herbs are at their most powerful shortly before flowering.

● Always pick and prepare herbs shortly before consumption.

● Never chop herbs too finely as the important etheric oils will be lost through evaporation.

● Healing herbs contain many effective substances, so never "overdose" on them.

Herbs for cooking can be used plentifully.

● Herbal teas drunk for healing purposes should be used on a short-term basis (that is, three to four times daily) and for no longer than four weeks. Mixed herbal teas, including those drunk daily, can be used for longer periods of time. It is a good idea to vary the herbal mixtures frequently.

● Caution is recommended with the consumption of herbs during pregnancy (see pp. 14-25).

**Herb quark** can be prepared according to the same recipe but add a finely chopped shallot to this mix.

**Herbal soups** will taste quite different depending on the ingredients added. A chervil soup is particularly delicious but other herbal mixes are good too.

● Basic recipe: one or two shallots lightly cooked in butter, add hot vegetable stock, chopped herbs and allow to come to the boil very briefly. Enhance with single cream.

● Finely puréed potato soup is a rare delicacy when mixed with finely chopped herbs. Garnish with flowers.

**Desserts** can also be enhanced with herbs. Among the "sweet" herbs are lemon thyme, lemon balm, basil, sweet Cicely and angelica. Try these recipes:

● cherry jam with finely chopped mint

● blackberry jelly with basil

● peach preserve with hyssop

● gooseberry or rhubarb preserve will acquire a milder flavour with the addition of the leaves and finely chopped stalks of sweet Cicely. Add these at the end and bring to the boil only briefly.

# Using herbs

### Herbs for health and well-being

When freshly picked and prepared, herbs can be an important nutritional supplement in healthy eating. In addition to vitamins and minerals, they also contain natural oils as well as antibacterial agents. They encourage proper digestion and the production of hormones, support the healing of wounds and generally increase resistance to illness.
**NB:** These healing substances, just like many vitamins, are destroyed by heat so always try to use herbs on a fresh, daily basis!

### Herbs in teas

Fresh herb teas have an incomparably better flavour than dried ones. Try freezing a small supply of herbs for tea. Mint and lemon balm, in particular, are almost as good frozen as they are freshly picked.
For herbal teas with fresh herbs, reckon on three teaspoons chopped herbs per cup. If you are using dried herbs, you will only need one teaspoon per cup. Pour boiling water over the herbs and allow to draw for ten minutes.

### Herbs for your bath

If the dried herbs are not all used up during the winter, you can still utilize them in a pleasantly relaxing or invigorating bath.
● Lemon balm has a relaxing effect.
● Rosemary is refreshing and invigorating.
● Oregano and thyme can be used as a cold preventive and for alleviating symptoms if you have a cold coming on.
**My tip:** 50-100 g (1¾-3½ oz) dried herbs in a small linen sack hung in the bath will prevent bits of herbs from floating in the water.

### Scented herbal posies

Fresh or dried herbal posies can cheer you throughout the year.
● Tarragon, angelica, fennel flowers, rue and St. John's wort stay fresh for a remarkably long time. The tough leaves of angelica make a good base for many bouquets.
● Suitable for drying: sage, santolina, yarrow, St. John's wort, rue (seedheads) and chamomile.
● Roses and herbs make as good partners in a vase as in the flowerbed. Wild roses and their hips harmonize well with rustic herbs. Flowering wormwood looks very effective with white roses.

● The seedheads of *Allium fistulosum* and chives are as attractive as ornamental leeks and their spherical shapes are very well suited to round posies.
● Rustic vases are effective for displaying herbs. Classic clear or coloured glass vases are also attractive with herb arrangements. Herbs retain a rural charm if arranged in baskets. Stand them in a glass jar containing water.
● Even in the kitchen you can use the herbs intended for cooking in a decorative way. A fat bunch of seasoning herbs arranged in a plump round vase will look mouthwatering when fresh: try parsley, salad burnet, mint, oregano, nasturtium and chives.
**My tip:** A bunch of herbs grown in your own garden also makes a fine gift when visiting friends. A very original present would consist of a bunch of herbs accompanied by a recipe for a salad using the herbs, a salad bowl and the necessary oil and vinegar.

*Sky blue borage flowerheads trapped in ice cubes served in summery Campari soda.*

## Herbal essences for the winter

Pot-pourris made of dried flowers and herbs can be bought ready-made almost everywhere now but creating your own, individual mixture is definitely more fun. This is my own recipe for a herb garden pot-pourri:

● Fill a 1 litre (1¾ pt) vessel to the brim with dried herb flowers and leaves, for example lavender, rosemary, mint, lemon balm, also rose petals and buds.

● Add dried lemon peel, marigold and chamomile flowers.

● Grind half a teaspoon each of cinnamon powder, angelica seed, coriander and cloves in a mortar.

● Add 25 g (¾ oz) violet root powder (from chemists) for fixing, plus a few drops of rose oil and lavender oil to the other ingredients in a bowl and mix well.

● Allow to stand for four weeks, then divide among separate bowls.

# Using herbs

A flowering bouquet in many colours is made up of yellow marigolds, the lilac racemes of apple mint, orange nasturtium flowers, yellow fennel umbels and sage and angelica leaves.

# Index

# Index

## Acknowledgements

The photographer and publishers wish to thank the following garden owners, nurseries and public institutions for their support and help:
Alderley Grange, Alderley, Wotton-under-Edge, Gloucestershire, England
Staudengartnerei Arends, Wuppertal, Germany
Madeleine van Bennekom, Domburg, Netherlands
Botanischer Garten, Munich, Germany
Mr and Mrs Caesar, Herten, Germany
Ineke Greve, Heerlen, Netherlands
Mr and Mrs Groenewegen, Beugen, Netherlands
Gruga Park, Essen, Germany
Hatfield House, Hatfield, Hertfordshire, England
Mr and Mrs Poley, Nisse, Netherlands
Mr and Mrs Rau, Bonen, Germany Westfalenpark, Dortmund, Germany
Westpark, Munich, Germany

## Author's note

This volume is concerned with the care and use of herbs. Most of the species discussed here should not be consumed in excess and other species also require some caution. The brief descriptions on pages 14-25 give details of any restrictions in respect to consumption under the keyword "Warning". Some plants secrete substances that can irritate the skin. This is also indicated in the relevant section. If you have a sensitive skin or are prone to contact allergies, you should make sure to wear gloves when handling these plants. Many of the herbs discussed here are not only for use in cooking but can also be employed in the preparation of herbal teas. Any long-term therapies using herbs should only be undertaken following the advice of a doctor familiar with herbal medicine.
If you suffer any injuries while in contact with soil, you should consider consulting a physician to discuss the possibility of a tetanus vaccination. All fertilizers and plant protection agents, even biological ones, should be stored where they are inaccessible to children or domestic pets. Consumption of these substances may lead to considerable harm to health. Also, do not allow these substances to come into contact with the eyes.

## Photographic acknowledgements

All of the photographs in this volume are by Marion Nickig with the exception of:
Cover photography by L. Rose.
Marktanner: p. 3 right; Mein Schöner Garten/Gross: p. 10; Silvestris/Sauer: p. 5 right; Skogstad: p. 43 right; Zepf: p. 45.

### Cover photographs

*Front cover: Lavender walk, balm, coriander and spearmint.*
*Inside front cover: "Jackman's Blue", a compact variety of rue, here used for edging a roundel.*
*Inside back cover: marigolds and lavender.*
*Back cover: A formal herb garden.*

This edition published 1995 by Merehurst Limited
Ferry House, 51-57 Lacy Road, Putney, London SW15 1PR
Reprinted 1996, 1998, 1999

© 1992 Gräfe und Unzer GmbH, Munich

ISBN 1 85391 533 5

A catalogue record for this book is available from the British Library.

English text copyright © Merehurst Limited 1995
*Translated by* Astrid Mick
*Edited by* Lesley Young
*Design and typesetting by* Paul Cooper

*Printed in Hong Kong by* Wing King Tong

Alderley Grange is a herb garden in England. Here, spherical privet trees and a large container of flowering nasturtiums catch the eye. The delicate leaves, slender stalks and inconspicuous flowers require such a classical framework to create a special effect.